Feagin, Clairece Booher.
Angry Feelings /

c199
33305222949895
gi   09/05/12   ;

Stories for Parents

Angry Feelings

CLAIRECE FEAGIN

Project Editor
Sarah Ann Schmidt

RETURN TO:

The Reading Program
(408) 262-1349

CB
CONTEMPORARY
BOOKS
CHICAGO

Library of Congress Cataloging-in-Publication Data

Feagin, Clairece Booher.
    Angry feelings / Clairece Feagin
       p.   cm.
    ISBN 0-8092-4141-2
    1. Child rearing—United States—Problems, exercises,
etc.   2. Anger.   I. Title.   II. Series.
HQ769.F283   1990
649'.1—dc20   90-15038
                                       CIP

Copyright © 1990 by Clairece Feagin
All rights reserved

No part of this publication may be reproduced, stored in a
retrieval system, or transmitted in any form or by any means,
without the prior written permission of the publisher.

Published by Contemporary Books, Inc.
180 North Michigan Avenue, Chicago, Illinois 60601
Manufactured in the United States of America
International Standard Book Number: 0-8092-4141-2

Published simultaneously in Canada by
Fitzhenry & Whiteside
91 Granton Drive, Richmond Hill, Ontario L4B 2N5 Canada

Clairece Feagin has an Ed.M. in elementary education from
Harvard University and has authored texts in the areas of child
development and social studies.

Jan Spivey Gilchrist was the 1989 recipient of the Coretta Scott
King Award for illustration.

Stories for Parents was evaluated and field-tested by the staff
and students at the National Center for Family Literacy in
Louisville, Kentucky.

Consultants: Meta Potts, Director of Adult Learning Services •
Bonnie Lash Freeman, Director of Early Childhood Services

Field-testers: Jennifer Whitehead • Louise Schulman • Susan
Henderson

Editorial Director: Caren Van Slyke

Editorial: Mark Boone • Sarah Conroy • Chris Benton • Lynn
McEwan

Cover Design and Illustrations: Jan Spivey Gilchrist

Art & Production: Lois Koehler

Table of Contents

Rainy days are hard for children.
They are also hard for parents when
children must stay indoors. What
are some safe indoor activities for
children?

The Lamp

Every day after their nap, Bill and John like to play in the yard. The brothers like to be outdoors. They like the warm sun and the cool air.

Sometimes Bill and John play alone. Sometimes a friend comes to play. Bill and John have many friends.

On rainy afternoons, the boys cannot go outdoors. They must stay indoors to play. Sometimes they get very tired of being indoors.

One rainy afternoon Bill and his friend Niki were playing with a ball indoors.

"Roll the ball on the floor," Mrs.

Carter told the children. "I don't want the ball to break anything."

"OK," said Bill. "We'll roll the ball on the floor."

"Get the ball," Niki shouted, and she rolled the ball across the floor.

"I want to play, too," John said.

Bill and Niki did not listen.

"I want to play, too!" John said in a loud voice.

Bill rolled the ball to Niki. Niki rolled the ball to Bill.

"Let me play, too!" John shouted. John grabbed the ball and ran.

"Give it back!" Niki yelled.

"We are playing with it. Give it back!" Bill shouted.

Bill and Niki ran after John. Niki grabbed the ball from John's hands. She threw it to Bill. But Bill did not catch the ball. The ball crashed into a lamp. The lamp fell to the floor and broke. Mrs. Carter felt very angry.

What are some other feelings Mrs. Carter probably had?

Think About the Story

(More than one answer may be right.)

1. Is it OK for Mrs. Carter to feel angry?

   (Yes. Almost anyone would feel angry if this happened, unless it was a lamp they hated!)

2. *How* should Mrs. Carter show her anger?

   ❏ **a.** scream at the children
   ❏ **b.** tell them they are bad
   ❏ **c.** spank the children
   ❏ **d.** tell them Mr. Carter will be angry
   ❏ **e.** tell them they can't have their afternoon snack
   ❏ **f.** calmly tell the children that she feels angry that the lamp broke
   ❏ **g.** let the children help clean up the mess

   (Answers *f* and *g* are good to do.)

4

Why are these answers right?

f. "calmly tell the children that she feels angry that the lamp broke"

Tell children the truth about how you feel. Even if you are angry, it is important to let children know how you feel about what they do.

Be sure to stay calm. This shows that you can feel anger and still keep your self-control. Children do what they see others do. The best way to teach children self-control is for you to show self-control.

Telling the truth about your feelings teaches children to trust you. It shows that you think the children are important. It shows that you respect the children. It helps the children respect you.

5

Talking about your feelings also teaches children to understand their own feelings. It teaches them to tell the truth about their *own* feelings.

≈

g. "let the children help clean up the mess"

It is good for children to help clean up a mess they make. Cleaning up helps children think about what they did. Tell them you are angry at what they *did,* not at them.

The children *did* something to make you angry. Now they can *do* something to help make things right between themselves and you.

Have children do what is safe. In this case, they can bring the broom and the dust pan. Children should not clean up broken glass.

Why are the other answers wrong?

a. "scream at the children"

Children do what they see others do. If you scream at the children, they will learn to scream at people when they are angry. Tell the children how you feel. But tell them calmly.

b. "tell them they are bad"

Talk about what the children did. Do not tell children they are bad. Show anger at the *act*, not at the child.

c. "spank the children"

Spanking or hitting a child is not a good way to show anger. It shows that you have lost your self-control. It shows children that hitting is OK.

d. "tell them Mr. Carter will be angry"

Talk about *your* feelings. Don't talk about someone else's feelings. Speak only for yourself.

e. "tell them they can't have their afternoon snack"

Taking food from children is not a good way to show anger. If the children break a lamp with a ball, you might take away the ball for a while. What you take away should have something to do with what the children did.

≈

Did you choose answers *f* and *g*?

Did you choose any of the wrong answers (*a, b, c, d,* or *e*)? If so, think about your reasons.

3. *When* should Mrs. Carter show her anger?

- ☐ **a.** the minute the lamp breaks
- ☐ **b.** as soon as she can keep her self-control after the lamp breaks
- ☐ **c.** every day for the next week (Answer *b* is good to do.)

Why is answer *b* right?

b. "as soon as she can keep her self-control after the lamp breaks."

Show your anger while the children remember what happened so they will understand what made you angry.

Don't show your anger before you can keep your self-control. Children learn self-control by seeing adults use self-control. Children learn to do what they see you do. Your actions are their best teacher. If you do not use self-control, it will be hard for your children to learn to use self-control.

≈

Why are the other answers wrong?

a. "the minute the lamp breaks"

Show your anger while the children still remember what they did. But wait until you can be calm. Do not show anger until you can keep your self-control.

c. "every day for the next week"

Deal with a problem when it happens. Then forget it. Children feel guilty enough when parents are angry.

What Happened?

Everyone feels anger sometimes — adults and children of all ages. Angry feelings frighten children. They need to learn that it is OK to feel anger, and they need to learn safe ways to show anger.

Children learn ways to show anger by seeing how their parents show anger. Here are some ways to be a good model for children:

- Keep your self-control.

- Be honest about how you feel.

- Tell the child you are angry about *what happened*, not at the child.

Many people show anger by hitting.
Do you think this is a good way to
show anger? Why or why not?

No Hitting Here

"I like to play at your house," Wanda told Tracy as the girls walked home.

"Hello, girls," Mrs. Carter said. "How was school?"

"Hi, Mom," Tracy said. "School was OK."

"Hello, Mrs. Carter," Wanda said.

"We're going to play horses," Tracy told her mother.

Mrs. Carter smiled. Model horses were the girls' favorite toys these days.

"Let's get some apples first," Tracy said.

"Good idea," answered Wanda. "Then give me the white horse that I left here last week."

"I lost that horse," Tracy said. "I'm sorry, Wanda. I'll look some more. Maybe we can find it."

"Lost it? How could you?" Wanda stood up and began to shout. "You're my best friend! How could you lose my horse? It was my best one!"

"I didn't mean to lose it," Tracy said. "It was just a horse. I'll buy you another one. Don't get so mad."

"Some friend you are," Wanda shouted, coming toward Tracy. "You don't care about my things. You don't care how I feel." Wanda raised her arm to hit Tracy.

"You can't hit in this house," Tracy shouted.

"Can you yell?" Wanda shouted back.

"If you have to," Tracy shouted, "you can yell."

"At our house, we hit," shouted Wanda.

"Do you like to hit?" asked Tracy.

"Yes," shouted Wanda. "When I am angry, I like to hit."

"Do you like to get hit?" asked Tracy.

"No, silly!" shouted Wanda. "Of course not. No one likes to get hit."

Wanda stopped shouting. She sat down. She got very quiet.

"No, I don't like to get hit," she said again, softly.

"Have you ever been hit?" Tracy asked.

"Sometimes when my dad is angry, he hits me," Wanda said. "Sometimes when my mom is angry, she hits me. I have been hit a lot," she added.

"What are you girls up to?" Mrs. Carter asked as she came into the room.

"We had a fight," Tracy said.

"Are you still angry?" Mrs. Carter asked.

"I don't think so," Tracy said. "I hope Wanda's not still mad at me. I'm sorry I lost her horse. I want to get her another one."

Wanda turned to Mrs. Carter. "Does anyone in this house ever hit?" she asked Mrs. Carter.

Mrs. Carter looked at Wanda kindly.

"No," said Mrs. Carter. "We don't believe in hitting. Hitting hurts. It doesn't help. Sometimes we may feel like hitting when we are

17

angry. But we try to show our anger in other ways."

"We talk to each other about how we feel," Mrs. Carter told Wanda. "We tell each other why we are angry. We try to understand how the other person feels."

"Some people hit when they are angry. They think it will make them

feel better. I don't think it does. When you hit someone, you hurt them. Then you feel sorry. You don't feel better. Then you may be angry at yourself because you hurt someone," Mrs. Carter said.

"Everyone gets angry. I get angry. Tracy gets angry. Tracy's dad gets angry. But we try to show our anger in other ways."

"I'd like things to work like that at my house," Wanda said.

"Maybe you and your mother could talk to someone who helps families show anger without hurting anyone," said Mrs. Carter.

"Uh, I don't know," said Wanda. "My mom might be mad that I told someone."

Mrs. Carter reached for the phone book. "You don't have to decide today, Wanda. Just remember that you can get help if you need it."

≈

Use the space below to write what you think Wanda should do.

Think About the Story

(More than one answer may be right.)

1. Why was Wanda angry?

- ❑ **a.** Wanda lost her own favorite horse.
- ❑ **b.** Her mother wouldn't let her go to Tracy's house.
- ❑ **c.** Tracy lost Wanda's favorite horse.

2. What did Wanda start to do?

- ❑ **a.** Hit Tracy.
- ❑ **b.** Go home.
- ❑ **c.** Take Tracy's horse.

3. How did Wanda feel about being hit?

- ❑ **a.** She didn't like to be hit.
- ❑ **b.** She'd like a "no hitting" rule at her house.
- ❑ **c.** She thought hitting was the best way to show anger.

4. What did Mrs. Carter tell Wanda?

    ❑ **a.** In this house we hit when we feel like it.

    ❑ **b.** Hitting doesn't help. We try to show our anger in other ways.

    ❑ **c.** We talk to each other about why we are angry.

_____

- Why did Mrs. Carter want Wanda's mother to talk with someone who helps families? How did Wanda feel about this?

- How could Wanda try to change the way her family shows anger?

_____

Right Answers: 1. c **2.** a **3.** a and b **4.** b and c

What Happened?

Most people show anger the same way their parents did. For many people, this means hitting.

Hitting doesn't show self-control. Hitting does not make things better. Hitting only hurts and makes people even angrier.

Mrs. Carter believed that when parents show anger they should also let children know they are still loved. She helped Wanda learn that there are better ways to deal with anger than by hitting.

What are some ways that parents
can help brothers and sisters end
fights with each other?

Bill's New Truck

Bill got a new truck for his birthday. He liked the new truck and played with it every day. Sometimes Bill let his brother John play with his new truck. But most of the time Bill wanted to play with his new truck himself.

"I want to play with your new truck," John told Bill one day.

"Well, OK," Bill told him. "But be careful. Don't hurt it."

John took Bill's truck outdoors. He pushed the truck on the sidewalk. He made the truck go very fast. John had fun playing with Bill's new truck.

"Does anyone want some juice?" Mrs. Carter called from the kitchen.

"I do," shouted John, and he ran into the house.

While John was in the house, it began to rain. Bill's new truck was still outside. John forgot about Bill's truck.

The next morning Bill looked for his new truck.

"Where's my truck?" Bill asked John.

"I don't know," John said.

"You played with it yesterday," Bill told John.

"Where did you play with Bill's truck?" Mrs. Carter asked John.

"On the sidewalk," John answered.

"Did you leave Bill's truck out in the rain?" Mrs. Carter asked John.

"My new truck!" Bill shouted as he ran outdoors. John ran after him. Mrs. Carter followed.

Bill found his new truck. It was wet and dirty. Bill felt very angry. He picked up the truck and started to hit John with it.

What should Mrs. Carter do?

- ❑ **a.** Let Bill hit John with the truck.
- ❑ **b.** Hit John herself.
- ❑ **c.** Hit Bill and John.
- ❑ **d.** Tell John he is bad for leaving the truck in the rain.
- ❑ **e.** Tell Bill not to be angry.
- ❑ **f.** Help Bill and John talk about how they feel.

(Answer *f* is good to do.)

Mrs. Carter put one hand on Bill's arm. She put her other hand on the truck.

"It's not OK to hit John," Mrs. Carter told Bill. "It's *never* OK to hit people. Let's sit on the porch and talk about how we feel."

"I'm *mad!*" Bill shouted, and he ran to the porch.

"That's OK," Mrs. Carter told him. "I understand. It's OK to feel angry. I would feel angry if someone left something of mine in the rain. But hitting John is not OK."

"How do you feel, John?" Mrs. Carter asked.

John began to cry. "I'm sorry I forgot about the truck. I'm sorry I left it in the rain," he said.

Bill looked at the truck. He wiped it with his hand.

"Let's clean your truck off," Mrs. Carter said. "John, will you get a rag? You can help Bill wipe the water off his truck. You can help Bill wipe the dirt from his truck. Then Bill's truck will look nice again. I think it will look as good as new."

Think About the Story

(More than one answer may be right.)

1. Why was Bill angry?

- ❑ **a.** He lost his new truck.
- ❑ **b.** John broke Bill's new truck.
- ❑ **c.** John left Bill's new truck in the rain.

2. Why did John leave Bill's new truck in the rain?

- ❑ **a.** He wanted to make Bill angry.
- ❑ **b.** He forgot about the truck.
- ❑ **c.** He wanted to ruin Bill's truck.

3. How did Bill feel when he found his truck wet and dirty?

- ❑ **a.** Bill felt angry.
- ❑ **b.** Bill didn't care.
- ❑ **c.** Bill asked for another new truck.

4. What did Mrs. Carter do?

☐ **a.** She told Bill to forget about the truck.

☐ **b.** She spanked John for leaving Bill's truck in the rain.

☐ **c.** She talked to her two boys and helped them understand their feelings.

☐ **d.** She let John help clean the truck.

• Why did Mrs. Carter tell Bill that he couldn't hit John?

• What did Mrs. Carter do that was good? Would you have done anything differently?

• What did your parents do when you had a fight with your brothers or sisters?

Right Answers: **1.** c **2.** b **3.** a
   4. c and d

Use this page to write about a fight your children have had with each other (or with a friend). What did you do to help them end the fight? Would you handle it differently today? Why or why not?

What Happened?

Brothers and sisters often get angry with each other. If their parents have been good models, children can learn safe, helpful ways to deal with angry feelings.

Mrs. Carter helped Bill and John by talking with them about how they felt. She let Bill know that it was OK to feel angry. She also helped Bill understand how John felt. Bill didn't feel so angry when he understood that John was sorry and didn't mean to hurt Bill's truck.

Then Mrs. Carter helped John find a way to show Bill he was sorry — John helped Bill clean the truck.

With a little help from a parent,
children can often answer their own
questions.

Jud's Father

"Mom, do you love me?" John asked Mrs. Carter.

"Of course I love you, John," Mrs. Carter answered, giving John a big hug. "You know I love you lots and lots and lots."

"You never hit me," John said. "Jud's dad hits him a lot. He says it's because he loves Jud."

"I see," said Mrs. Carter. "Would you like for me to hit you?"

"Not really," John answered. "But Jud says parents are supposed to hit children if they really love them."

"Do you believe Jud is right?" Mrs. Carter asked.

John thought a bit. "I don't know," he finally said.

"Do you like to play with Jud?" Mrs. Carter asked.

"No!" John answered quickly. "He's mean. He's a bully. He's always hitting everyone."

"Why do you think he hits so much?" Mrs. Carter asked.

"I don't know," John answered.

"I think maybe he hits other children because he gets hit so much himself," Mrs. Carter told John.

"How do you feel when Jud hits you?" she asked.

"Mad," John said. "*Really* mad."

"Do you think Jud feels angry

when his father hits him?" Mrs. Carter asked.

"I don't know. Jud says his father hits him because he loves him," John said. "If his father loves him, Jud shouldn't be angry."

"But you get angry when you are hit. Would you be angry if I hit you or if your father hit you?" Mrs. Carter asked.

"I guess I would," John said.

"Last week you marked on the wall in your room. I wasn't happy about it, but I didn't hit you," Mrs. Carter said.

"You told me you didn't like it. And you told me why you didn't like it. You told me it was better to mark on paper. Then you made me wash the marks off the wall," John said.

"If I were Jud's father, I guess I would have hit you," Mrs. Carter told John.

"I'll say," John answered. "Jud would have gotten a really bad one

for that. Jud gets hit for everything —
for coming home late, for getting in
trouble at school, for lying."

"What do you think Jud learns
when his father hits him? Does he
stop coming home late? Does he stop
getting in trouble at school?" Mrs.
Carter asked.

"No," John told her.

"Why do you think Jud lies?" Mrs.
Carter asked.

"Maybe so his father won't catch
him doing things and hit him," John
said.

"Do you think you would have
learned not to write on the walls if I
had hit you?" Mrs. Carter asked.

John didn't answer.

"I think you would only have gotten angry. Then you might have wanted to hit someone else," Mrs. Carter told John.

"Hitting hurts. Hitting doesn't show love. Hitting shows anger."

"Then why does Jud's father hit him?" John asked.

"Jud's father must feel a lot of anger. Maybe he doesn't know any other way to show his anger but to hit," Mrs. Carter said.

"Do you think Jud's father loves him?" John asked.

"I'm sure he does," Mrs. Carter said. "But he doesn't have a very good way of showing it. Maybe Jud's father got hit when he was a child. Maybe that's the only way he knows to deal with children. But I don't think it is a very good way. In fact, I think it is a bad way."

John put his arms around his mother. "I'm glad you love me," John told her. "And I'm glad you don't hit me."

Think About the Story

(More than one answer may be right.)

1. Why did John ask Mrs. Carter if she loved him?

   ❑ **a.** She had just hit him.
   ❑ **b.** She never hit him.
   ❑ **c.** Jud told John that parents are supposed to hit children if they love them.

2. Mrs. Carter thought that

   ❑ **a.** Jud's father was right to hit Jud.
   ❑ **b.** all children need to be hit.
   ❑ **c.** hitting was a bad way to deal with children.

3. John told Mrs. Carter that when he got hit he felt

   ❑ **a.** angry.
   ❑ **b.** loved.
   ❑ **c.** happy.

42

4. Mrs. Carter thought Jud's father hit Jud because

- ☐ **a.** he didn't know any other way to deal with children.
- ☐ **b.** he didn't love Jud.
- ☐ **c.** this was the best way to deal with a bully like Jud.

- Why do you think Jud was a bully to other children?

- Do you think that hitting children is a helpful way to deal with problems? What do you think is the best way for parents to deal with children when they disobey?

Right Answers: **1.** b and c **2.** c
3. a **4.** a

43

Getting Help

For some families, hitting becomes a way of life. No one in these families is happy. These families need help.

Many cities have special phone numbers to call to get help for such families. Find out what help your city or town has and write the numbers here:

Child Abuse Hotline

_____

Parents' Hotline

_____

(sometimes called *Parents' Helpline* or *Parents' Warmline*)